D0594349

Giftbooks in this series by Helen Exley:
Words on Hope   Words on Joy
Words on Courage   Words on Kindness
Words of Wisdom   Words on Love and Caring

Published simultaneously in 1997 by Exley Publications in
Great Britain, and Exley Giftbooks in the USA.
Copyright © Helen Exley 1997
The moral right of the author has been asserted.

12 11 10 9 8 7 6

Edited and pictures selected by Helen Exley
ISBN 1-85015-921-1

Picture research by Image Select International.
Typeset by Delta, Watford.
Printed in China.

**Exley Publications Ltd, 16 Chalk Hill, Watford,
Herts WD1 4BN, UK.
Exley Publications LLC, 232 Madison Avenue,
Suite 1206, NY 10016, USA.**

Words of Wisdom

A HELEN EXLEY
GIFTBOOK

EXLEY
NEW YORK • WATFORD, UK

It had been my repeated experience
that when you said to life
calmly and firmly (but very firmly!)

"I trust you; do what you must,"
life had an uncanny way of
responding to your need.

OLGA ILYIN

A tree
that reaches past
your embrace grows
from one small seed.
A structure over
nine stories high begins
with a handful of earth.
A journey of
a thousand miles starts
with a single step.

TAO 64

Nothing great is created suddenly, any more than a bunch of grapes or a fig. If you tell me that you desire a fig, I answer you that there must be time. Let it first blossom, then bear fruit, then ripen.

EPICTETUS

*There are
no shortcuts
to any place
worth going.*

There is so much in the world
for us all if we only have
the eyes to see it, and the heart

*to love it, and the hand
to gather it to ourselves....*

LUCY MAUD MONTGOMERY
(1874-1942)

Be the change
you want to see
in the world.

MAHATMA GANDHI
(1869-1948)

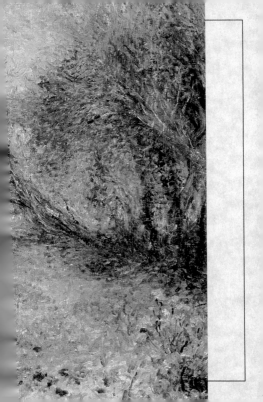

To compose our character
is our duty....
Our great and glorious
masterpiece is to live
appropriately.
All other things, to rule,
to lay up treasure, to build,
are at most but little
appendices and props....

MICHEL DE MONTAIGNE
(1533-1592)

From success you get lots
of things, but not that great
inside thing that
love brings you.

SAM GOLDWYN

In this world there is nothing
softer or thinner than water.
But to compel the hard and
unyielding, it has no equal.
That the weak overcomes
the strong, that the hard gives
way to the gentle –
This everyone knows, yet no one
acts accordingly.

LAO-TZU
(6TH CENTURY B.C.)

He who smiles
rather than rages is always
the stronger.

JAPANESE WISDOM

This is what knowledge really is. It is finding out something for oneself with pain, with joy, with exultancy, with labor, and with all the little ticking, breathing moments of our lives, until it is ours as that only is ours which is rooted in the structure of our lives.

THOMAS WOLFE
(1900-1938)

Do not fear going
forward slowly,
fear only to stand still.

CHINESE
WISDOM

Our lives are like
the course of the sun.
At the darkest moment
there is the promise
of daylight.

LONDON "TIMES" EDITORIAL,
DECEMBER 24, 1984

Only one principle
will give you courage, that is
the principle that no evil
lasts forever nor indeed for
very long.

EPICURUS
(3 4 1 - 2 7 1   B . C .)

KINDNESS IS MORE
IMPORTANT THAN WISDOM,
AND THE RECOGNITION
OF THIS IS THE BEGINNING
OF WISDOM.

THEODORE
ISAAC
RUBIN

KIND WORDS

CAN BE SHORT

AND EASY TO SPEAK,

BUT THEIR ECHOES

ARE ENDLESS.

MOTHER TERESA, b 1910

We don't have to be facing
a personal tragedy to make
our relationships our number
one priority.
No project, no deadline,
no clean kitchen is as
important as the quality
of our relationships.

FROM
"RANDOM ACTS OF KINDNESS"

If you've only one
breath left,
use it to say thank you.

PAM BROWN.
b. 1928

I f all men
were to bring
their miseries
together
in one place,
most would
be glad to take
each his own
home again
rather than
take a portion
out of the
common stock.

SOLON
(638-559 B.C.)

NOT TO DO HONOUR TO OLD AGE
IS TO DEMOLISH IN THE MORNING
THE HOUSE WHEREIN WE ARE TO
SLEEP AT NIGHT.

ALPHONSE KARR

To know
how to grow old
is the master-work
of wisdom,
and one of the most
difficult chapters in
the great art
of living.

HENRI
FREDERIC
AMIEL

THE GREATEST

REVELATION

IS STILLNESS.

LAO-TZU
(6TH CENTURY B.C.)

Better than a thousand
useless words
is one single word
that gives peace.

THE DHAMMAPADA

HAPPINESS

IS WHEN WHAT YOU THINK,

WHAT YOU SAY,

AND WHAT YOU DO

ARE IN HARMONY.

MAHATMA GANDHI
(1869-1948)

Because we are mortal, every talent, skill, ability we possess, every thought and feeling we ever have, every beautiful sight we ever see, every material possession we own, will ultimately be lost.
Unless we share it.
Unless we give what we have to others — to our spouse, to our child, to our friends and neighbors, to the strangers we encounter on our path — what we know and value will be irrevocably and utterly gone.

THE EDITORS OF CONARI PRESS, FROM "THE PRACTICE OF KINDNESS"

Only in growth,

reform and change,

paradoxically enough,

is true security

to be found.

ANNE MORROW LINDBERGH, *b*.1906

Never bear more than one kind of trouble at a time. Some people bear three — all they have had, all they have now, and all they expect to have.

EDWARD EVERELL HALE
(1822-1909)

That the birds of worry and care fly above your head, this you cannot change. But that they build nests in your hair, this you can prevent.

CHINESE PROVERB

Understanding, and action proceeding from understanding and guided by it, is the one weapon against the world's bombardment, the one medicine, the one instrument by which liberty, health, and joy may be shaped or shaped toward, in the individual, and in the race.

Neither man nor woman
can be worth anything
until they have discovered
that they are fools.

WILLIAM LAMB,
VISCOUNT MELBOURNE

Every man is a damn fool
for at least five minutes
every day;
Wisdom consists of not
exceeding that limit.

ELBERT HUBBARD

We're drowning in information and starving for knowledge.

RUTHERFORD D. ROGERS

Sometimes it proves the highest understanding not to understand.

BALTASAR GRACIÁN
(1601-1658)

Joy is not in things; it is in us.

RICHARD WAGNER
(1813-1883)

The most
evident token
and apparent
sign of true
wisdom is
a constant
and
unconstrained
rejoicing.

MICHEL DE
MONTAIGNE
(1533-1592)

The secret of happiness
is not doing what one likes
to do, but in liking
what one has to do.

SIR JAMES M. BARRIE
(1860-1937)

Many run about after
happiness like an
absent-minded man hunting for
his hat, while it is
in his hand
or on his head.

JAMES SHARP
(1613-1679)

Take time to be friendly —
It is the road to happiness.
Take time to dream —
It is hitching your wagon
to a star.
Take time to love
and to be loved —
It is the privilege of the gods.
Take time to look around —
It is too short a day to
be selfish.
Take time to laugh —
It is the music of the soul.

OLD ENGLISH PRAYER

In spite of all wanderings,
happiness is always found
within a narrow compass
and among objects which
lie within our immediate
reach.

BULWER

Without stirring abroad
one can know
the whole world;
Without looking out of
the window one can see
the way of heaven.
The further one goes
the less one knows.

LAO-TZU
(6TH CENTURY B C)

IF WE ARE

FACING

IN THE RIGHT

DIRECTION,

ALL WE

HAVE TO DO

IS TO KEEP

ON WALKING.

ANCIENT

BUDDHIST

EXPRESSION

K*nowledge is proud that he has learned so much; Wisdom is humble that he knows no more.*

WILLIAM COWPER
(1731-1800)

I want to beg you, as much as
I can, to be patient toward

all that is unsolved in your heart
and to try to love the questions
themselves like locked rooms
and like books that are written
in a very foreign tongue.
Do not seek the answers, which
cannot be given you because

you would not be able to live them.
And the point is to live everything.
Live the questions now.
Perhaps you will then gradually,
without noticing it, live along
some distant day into the answer.

RAINER MARIA RILKE
(1875-1926)

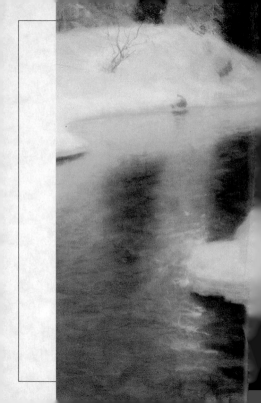

Freedom from desire
leads to inward peace.

LAO-TZU
(6TH CENTURY B.C.)

Our chief
want in life
is someone who
will make us do
what we can.

RALPH
WALDO
EMERSON
(1803-1882)

Treat people as if
they were what
they ought to be
and you will help them
become what they
are capable of becoming.

JOHANN WOLFGANG VON GOETHE
(1749-1832)

Trust [people], and they
will be true to you; treat
them greatly, and they will
show themselves great.

RALPH WALDO EMERSON
(1803-1882)

To laugh often and much;
to win the respect
of intelligent people
and the affection
of children;
to earn the appreciation
of honest critics
and endure the betrayal
of false friends.
To appreciate beauty;
to find the best in others;
to leave the world

a bit better
whether by a healthy child,
a garden patch or
a redeemed social condition;
to know that even
one life has breathed easier
because you have lived.
This is to have succeeded.

RALPH WALDO EMERSON
(1803-1882)

Learn from the past. Do not come to the end of your life only to find you have not lived. For many come to the point of leaving the space of the earth and when they gaze back, they see the joy and the beauty that could not be theirs because of the fears they lived.

CLEARWATER

Don't hurry, don't worry. You're only here for a short visit. So be sure to stop and smell the flowers.

WALTER HAGEN

When we forgive someone,
the knots are untied
and the past is released.

RESHAD FEILD

Grant to me that I may be made beautiful in my soul within, and that all external possessions be in harmony with my inner man.

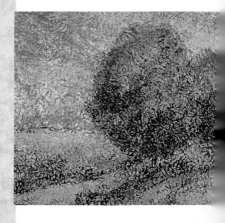

May I consider the wise man rich,
and may I have such wealth as
only the self-restrained man can
bear or endure.

SOCRATES (469-399 B.C.)

That it will
never come again
is what makes
life so sweet.

EMILY DICKINSON
(1830-1886)

Acknowledgements: The publishers are grateful for permission to reproduce copyright material. Whilst every effort has been made to trace copyright holders, the publishers would be pleased to hear from any not here acknowledged. EDITORS OF CONARI PRESS: Extract from *The Practice of Kindness* © 1996 The Editors of Conari Press. Extract from *Random Acts of Kindness,* © 1993 The Editors of Conari Press. Used with permission of Conari Press. LAO-TZU: Extracts reproduced by kind permission of Search Press Ltd, Wellwood, North Farm Road, Tunbridge Wells, Kent TN2 3DR.

Picture Credits: Exley Publications would like to thank the following organizations and individuals for permission to reproduce their pictures. Whilst every effort has been made to trace copyright holders, the publishers would be pleased to hear from any not here acknowledged. AISA, Art Resource (AR), Bridgeman Art Library (BAL), Edimedia (EDM), Fine Art Photographic Library (FAP), Image Bank, National Museum of American Art, Superstock (SS).
Cover and title page: © 1997 Patrick William Adam, *Interior, Morning,* BAL; page 6/7: © 1997 Harold Speed, *Alpine Landscape,* SS; page 9: © 1997 Louis Ritman, *Road to the Village;* page 11: Victor Moya, *Portrait of a Woman,* AISA; page 12/13: Vincent Van Gogh, *Field under thunderclouds;* page 14/15: Pierre Auguste Renoir, *Snow Landscape,* Giraudon/AR; page 16: Aime Perret, *Still Life with Flowers,* FAP;